a little book of poems

a little book of poems

love, regrets & redwoods

adam lambert

ISBN: 978-1-3999-6681-8

To Maisie, my love,
for whom my creativity flourishes;

&

To Granny,
for sharing your love of poetry with
me since I was born.

contents:

The Pilgrimage of a Union

Counting up the coppers
That you scraped from behind the sofa
To buy that pinstripe suit
The very best one you could find
At the charity shop

An old work shirt from back in the day
Oh weren't those the good times
A cheap second-hand tie
Nothing wrong with that
And some shoes from a skip

You catch a lift
Then another and another
Brave travellers with kind hearts
To finally arrive at that lowly town
And spend the night in a doorway

A pitiful whimper is drowned out
By moist lashings and wicked gusts
And threats of violence
Just please not the suit, you cry
Like that'll help

But it's all worth it, come the morning
With a brush down and clean up
For that momentary juncture
To see that veil and that rose
And those smiles

The Figure of the Night

Cool light rained down from the blackness
Piercing and still
The air was loud with silence
And felt heavy to the touch

An everlasting blanket journeyed to the horizon
The end of all things and the beginnings of anew
Droplets of dew clung on for dear life
Yet destined to succumb to gravity

The sleeping guardian ever-present
Casting its gaze over its home
The vacuum of calm broken only
By a solitary statue

Its silhouette loomed ominously
A lingering shadow of keratin and flesh
A fickle character
A wandering soul

But it stood firm amongst the assault of the night
Unfazed, unaltered
And returned to its herd
Beneath the light of the moon

Mother

A wild land,
A mystical realm

The benevolence of a thousand generations
Soaked into the earth underfoot

There was a calling to this place

There was a charm about it
A coy beauty

And yet its grace hosted only
The habitual activity

Of birds and of dragonflies,
Of ivy and of ferns

Pyre

The flickering of candlelight illumination,
A warm glow of safety in an otherwise desolate
blackness
Its dance was majestic and bold
Like a regal swan gliding over a Russian lake
Its golden mane - feared and prized,
Eternal yet momentary, exclusive yet omnipresent

The potential to dismember entire forests
But with the fragility of a single touch
The capacity to build, the capabilities to destroy
To begin revolutions, to start new eras

And yet, as the last drop of wax falls away
And the final inch of wick withers willingly,
The room is once again consumed
By the void of the nothing

Mistakes Too True

Cycling through the minds of the weary,
Pictures of the warmth of bonfire
Of tranquillity, of calm
Of what life used to be

But long gone are the scraps of that world
A brutal oasis corrupted by pain

Oh how they long for the sweet screech of blackbirds
The gruelling roar of traffic
Or the grating yells of market life

For now there is only a deafening silence
And where there once was life
Is now filled with nothing but regret.

Eternal Gratitude

Do the constellations that decorate the nights sky
Paint the same picture as the day they were named?
And has the roughness of oak bark endured
Since it was felt by only apes?

Does the sun that beats down upon us feel different
To the one that warmed the pharaohs, or the Aztecs?
And has the sweet scent of ferns mellowed
Since it was experienced by the builders of Rome?

But how can this vastness be comprehended
By those whose breath lasts but a second?
By those whose homes serve for mere years?
By those whose lives are important to so few in the universe?

For the grand redwoods care not for the comings and goings of Monday mornings
And the Atlantic knows not of its neighbours inhabiting the land

But although the Earth's breath aligns not with the days of man,
Nor do their hearts beat alike,
It stays hospitable and welcoming the best it knows how
And the stars still look down upon us and smile

Daytime Warfare

War rages.
A fierce war that endures faultlessly
Unrelenting and bold

It consumes the pride of even the most brazen of men
Exposing the scars of anguish from afar
A mundane warhead of familiar mediocrity

For the battles of this war deal not in the formalities
Of mortar shells and ammunition
But instead of pleasantries and of customs

Armed only with a grin,
The defences quake but cease to falter,
Barraged by the assault of the day

For the warmth of the eve is a welcome sight,
The safety of blackness comforting
At least until the discord of the day returns at dawn

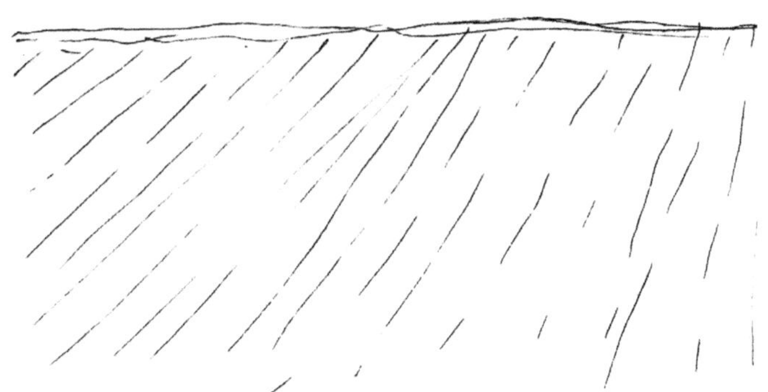

To My Doting Heart

A droplet of water on broken, parched lips
The crackling warmth of a mid-winter glow

A delicate arrangement of oils to a blank canvas
Or soothing gusts that complement the summer's heat

Adept strings attuned to the most beautiful of
symphonies
Roaming herds inhabiting pastures anew

Meanders of rivers married to steadfast banks
The aroma of wildflowers to a fair maiden's nose

Fall short in their entirety in beauty and in union
To you, my dear, and to my doting heart

Stones Before Me

Sometimes I sit and wonder
Where the stones before me have cast their gaze
Who's hands have brushed over their chiselled faces
What paths they have ventured down in another life.

But often I sit and wonder
Why I ponder on the stones before me
For they are here, as am I
And I need not know their distance pasts or long
forgotten lives

And yet I sit and wonder
Their scars offering teasing glimpses
Hints of courageous journeys
Battles eked out over centuries of conflict

So as I sit and wonder
I can only surrender in awe of their history
And let fleeting thoughts of fantasy pass by as just that
And revel in the knowledge of my uncertainty

For there is little to do but sit and wonder

Long Coats and Tote Bags

Parading around your sense of pride,
An embellishment garnished by every fibre of that coat
Never with more impetus than that moment
When the beauty of purpose graced your presence,
Met with the solemn charm of honesty, and the coyness
of peace

Every thread that swings blissfully alongside you,
A chance for new beginnings, an acknowledgment of the
now
This intertwined chaos may had once seemed futile,
An empty path leading to everywhere and nowhere

But now it sits joyously on your shoulder,
For the moment at least,
And will come to find its home on the rail,
Amongst the long coats and the tote bags

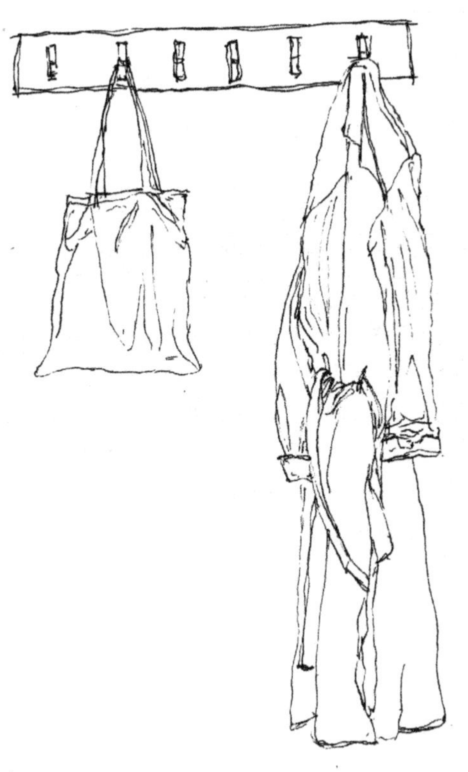

The Siege of The Botanicals

Oh how you try to remember what came before this life
Before you spent your waking hours engulfed in this
paradise
A glorious tragedy of foliage and stems
A comforting mossy pillow suffocating your every sinew

Fickle fenestrations offer but a fleeting flash of freedom
Before the terra cotta minefield once again rears its
head in rebellion
But as the fierce grip of roots tighten and the cacti
spikes stand defiant
You find peace in the knowledge that your body is home

And you once again can share your breath willingly
With the jungle prison and its loyal family

The Olive Tree

Visible cracks on aged skin, a tapestry of sorts
Or a map, perhaps
A diary of my reclusive years scrawled into flesh and
bark

My company kept to that of birdsong
And seldom trodden dirt
A peaceful life
Quiet, lonely

But often I wonder
Why this is so
And ponder on the mysteries
And revel in the facts

For I have not the grandeur of redwoods
Nor the might of oaks
I lack the grace of the willow
And the beauty of cherry blossom
The utility of maple alludes me
As does the maturity of pine

But do I not breathe the same air as my brothers?
Stand in the same soil that they call their own?
Does the same sun not feed us?
The same rain not quench our thirst?

So unalike others as I may be
There is still a place for my roots to burrow
A purpose for my being
A belonging
A home

The Night Before the Morning After

3 o'clock comes
We gather at the cupboard
Collect our tools
Filled with anticipation

It's a short drive
But it feels like an age
A stop off to reconvene
A short practice

The car's now full
An even shorter journey
A lay-by drop off
Hiding the car away after

An obligatory pub trip
Hope they don't ID
They haven't before
Into the garden

Time has come
Rush back to the fortress
So quiet
Oh but it won't be

Checks done
Feeling good
Excitement builds
Another quick tinny

The queue begins
We hide in waiting
We get the nod
The lights dim

The air's thick
Sweaty faces in the lights
A sticky floor
And a low ceiling

Me

Tiger stripes
Spattered freckles
Hereditary ptosis
And the odd scar

A crudely placed birthmark
A disability
Some hyper mobile joints
And some, stiff and sore

Dirty, bitten fingernails
Greasy hair
A permanent addiction to stimulation
Fallen arches

A catalogue of introspection
Of the body
And of the mind
Not to grieve
Or cry
Or even to blame
But to acknowledge
Appreciate
Love

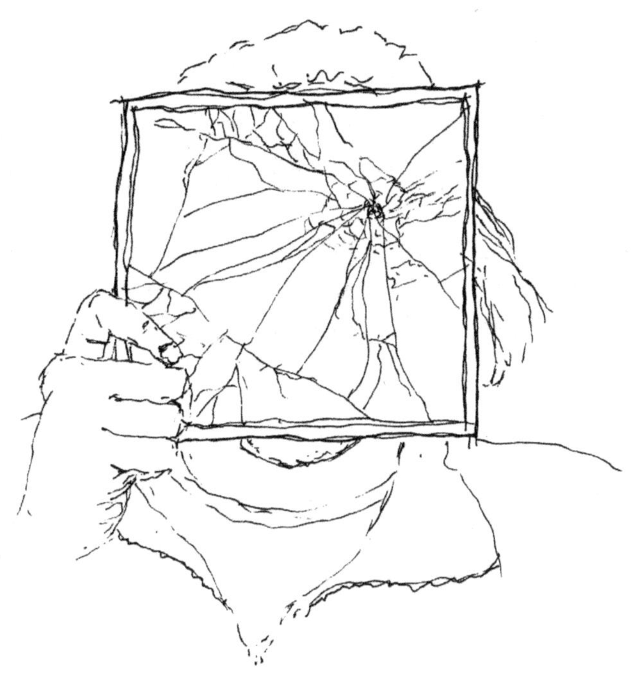

What Could Be

To whom it may concern
When did you give up
At what point did the profit margins
Exterminate the fear of losing yourself

Are you proud of your throne
That you sit atop of
Crafted from the ashes of your failure
Fuelled by desires of positive figures and upward graphs

Why did the green future you pitched fade to a dull grey
And who gave out the cost code for our sanity
To which company did you sell the air to
And the grass
And the trees
And the oceans
And the hope

Did you check with HR before abandoning our
prospects
Or did the orders come from corporate
With a 'we're sorry' card and a gas mask

Oh The Memories

I think it was daisies
No, petunias
Roses perhaps
Or maybe tulips

Dressed in red
Or blue or green or black

Actually it may have been sunflowers
Yes, I think it was

Her makeup was stunning
Well
I think she was wearing makeup
Or maybe not

We went out for hot chocolate
Or did you get a coffee
Or it could have been tea
Peppermint perhaps

But that smile
God, that smile
Imprinted in my memories
Like a polaroid

A Thursday Afternoon

Words on a screen
Ink on a page
Raindrops on a window
Casting shadows on a floor

A gentle breeze
Turning to a steady gust
A distant flash of feathers
The moon in a blue sky

A newspaper sprawled out
A stack of books
A kumquat tree
Contentment

The Scrutiny of the Flowerbeds

Upturned stones and parted bricks
Grasses gently pushed aside
Looking for a sign,
A glimmer, a trace

Sheltered nooks searched
Investigations persist
As the daffodils watch on
Bewildered

For they had not come across such curiosity
Not in the ways which occur before them
A meaningless hunt
Exploration to no avail

The petals of yellow and of white
Witness defeat on their doorstep
And the pursuit ceases
As two eyes peer on
From between the reeds

The Waiting Room

A quiet 5 minutes
In this bustling metropolis
A fortress of ancient red brick and mortar
With its lavish adornments
And living masterpieces

The soft magenta velvet
The crisp aged oak
The ornate white steelwork
The rugged stone

A quiet 5 minutes just to sit
A necessary wait
But peaceful all the same

The Lady of the House

Relics of a long forgotten age
Swept away with the wind are the lives of those
Who's footsteps echoed through those halls
Eroded are the coat hooks, the hat racks
And in their place sits depressed faces of stone and brick

The lodgings and lodgers exist only as myths
And the hunting party has withered away
But the evidence of their presence lingers on
Not in the steel and gunpowder they donned

But in the meadows
And the Saturday morning walks
In the laughter of newcomers
And the omnipresence of antlers

Sgwar Santes Anne

Donkey ride signs that take you back
To a time in which you need not worry
About who's paying for the chips
Or whether you've packed sun cream

The crowded streets that seemed so vast
Are now conquered in a short walk
But still you hear flashes of conversations
From the aged faces planted upon the benches

SGWAR SANTES ANNE
ST ANNE'S SQUARE

Theatr y Ddraig

The winged protector rests on high ground
Embossed in stone
Engrained in their culture
A pious beacon capped in slate
Punctured with ornamental light

Overlooked by slopes and ridges
Of gorse blankets and rocky peaks
Speckled with signs of ancient life
And hints of the future too
Through steel webs and timber clearings

But even still they find solace
In the cool embrace of tradition
Even if the many have now become the few
And scores of their chapels are no longer
The scaly beast stays with them
On their walls and in their hearts

Food Banks and Bentleys

They say they should stop playing politics
And go back to their mindless slog
Blame it on the people for being ill
As they travel in their Astons to their private check ups

Because there's loads of people saving lives
And only a handful of CEOs
They do so much, is what we're told
And it's not hard to try harder
To do more

They blame the poor for getting poorer
And making the banks look bad
Because it's not hard to batch cook for 14
When you have a chef to do it for you

For they have many fingers in many pies
Grubby fingers in stale pies
That they serve to their mutts
And to the people at the shelter

But people see through it now
And know it's not the lack of skills
"For the square root of f*** all
Is always going to be f*** all"

Between the Banks and the Marshland

What is minutia but the momentary divide
Between murky depths of stone and silt
And reed-strewn grasses
Offering no confidence of sure-footedness

A plethora of beautiful hazards
Sturdily poised in a pristine landscape
A joyous wasteland of bustling ecology
On-looked but seldom trodden

But somewhere on that perilous boundary
A window of opportunity lays beckoning
A slender strip of safety offering serene security
A place of contentment, contemplation, calm

Humility and Homes

A symphony of bricks and mortar
Baked into a page
Each ink streak blurring the lines
Between imagination and concrete

Enticing shapes with prestigious authority
Conjuring not only emotions
But rattles of bolts and screws
A chorus of screeching and rumbling

Like words of a script
Engrained in the memory of the finest actors
Recounted with charm and passion
At the precise juncture they were needed

Or the soirée of clefs and crotchets
Pulsating from viola strings
With such delicacy, subtlety
Capable from only the deftest touch and acute ear

La Renaissance de l'Âme

Were the delicate words of ode to be etched in a loving
face of hopeful slate
They would recount tales of your grace til they were
but dust

Or were the elegant strokes of pigmented oils to
capture but a fragment of your beauty
They would be marvelled at with such awe that even the
stoniest souls would be soothed

And still I find myself pondering on the truth that I call
my life, my love
Endlessly debating the notions that I may be hers and
she mine

For be it not in the bricks and mortar of our divide that
our souls lie
But comforted in the presence of the others company

Not housed in a dwelling or even a place but a feeling
Not tainted by the separation but jovial in their strength

For you, my love, compare not to any being in warmth,
or in compassion
Not only my world, my rock, but the one who's arms I
call home